Fact Finders™

The American Colonies

The Maryland Colony

by Mandy R. Marx

Capstone
press

Mankato, Minnesota

Fact Finders is published by Capstone Press,
151 Good Counsel Drive, P.O. Box 669, Mankato, Minnesota 56002.
www.capstonepress.com

Library of Congress Cataloging-in-Publication Data
Marx, Mandy R.
   The Maryland colony / by Mandy R. Marx.
   p. cm.—(Fact Finders. The American colonies)
   Includes bibliographical references and index.
   ISBN 0-7368-2675-0 (hardcover)
   1. Maryland—History—Colonial period, ca. 1600–1775—Juvenile literature. I. Title.
II. Series: American colonies (Capstone Press)
F184.M38 2006
975.2'02—dc22   2004029073

Summary: An introduction to the history, government, economy, resources, and people of
   the Maryland Colony. Includes maps and charts.

Editorial Credits
Katy Kudela, editor; Jennifer Bergstrom, set designer, illustrator, and book designer;
   Bobbi J. Dey, book designer; Kelly Garvin, photo researcher/photo editor

Photo Credits
Cover image: *Founding of the Colony of Maryland*, by Emanuel Gottlieb (1816–1866),
   SuperStock Inc.

Capstone Press Archives/The Colonial Williamsburg Foundation, 19; Corbis/Archivo
Iconografico, S.A., 4–5; Corbis/Bettmann, 12–13; Corbis/Lowell Georgia, 23; Courtesy of
Maryland Commission on Artistic Property of the Maryland State Archives, *The Burning of
the Peggy Stewart*, by Francis Blackwell Mayer (1827–1899), 26–27; Courtesy of Maryland
Commission on Artistic Property of the Maryland State Archives, *Founding of Maryland*, by
Tompkins Harrison Matteson (1813–1884) (detail), 20–21; Courtesy of Maryland State
Archives (detail), 14; The Granger Collection, New York, 7, 10, 11, 17, 29 (left); National
Archives and Records Administration, 29 (right); North Wind Picture Archives, 6, 15

**Capstone Press wishes to thank Mimi Calver, Director of Exhibits, Outreach, and Artistic Property
of the Maryland State Archives, Annapolis, Maryland, for her assistance with this project.**

1 2 3 4 5 6 10 09 08 07 06 05

Table of Contents

Chapter 1
Maryland's First People

In 1634, English settlers arrived in what is now Maryland. The English settlers were not the first people to live in Maryland. American Indians had lived there for thousands of years. There were different groups, but all spoke the Algonquian language.

Algonquian Daily Life

The Algonquian lived in wigwams made of wood. Wigwams had round roofs covered with bark. The Algonquian built wooden walls called **palisades** around their villages. Palisades protected the villages from enemy attacks and wild animals.

Groups of Algonquian lived together in villages.

▲ Algonquian Indians fished
in the Chesapeake Bay.

Algonquian Indians lived off the land. Women grew beans, corn, and squash. Men hunted and fished. The Algonquian ate fish and shellfish from the Chesapeake Bay. They used the shells as tools, jewelry, and money.

The Algonquian traded with nearby tribes. They traded their own goods and supplies for another tribe's tools, weapons, and food.

FACT!

The Algonquian hunted white-tailed deer for food. They used deerskins for clothing.

After English settlers arrived in 1634, the Algonquian traded with them. The settlers had metal tools and weapons. The Algonquian had furs that were valuable to people in England.

The Algonquian shared farming and hunting skills with the settlers. During the colony's early years, relations between the Algonquian and the settlers were friendly.

English settlers often traded with the Algonquian. ▼

~ Chapter 2 ~

Early Settlers

Maryland began as the dream of George Calvert, the first Lord Baltimore. Lord Baltimore was a Catholic living in England in the 1600s. At that time, Catholics could not worship in public. They could not hold government jobs.

Lord Baltimore wanted a place where Catholics would have better lives. He asked King Charles I of England for a **charter** to start an English colony in North America.

By the time the king granted the charter, Lord Baltimore had died. His son, Cecilius Calvert, the second Lord Baltimore, accepted the charter in 1632. He named his new colony Maryland.

Settlers started the Maryland Colony along the Chesapeake Bay. By 1763, the colony's borders reached west to the Appalachian Mountains. ➤

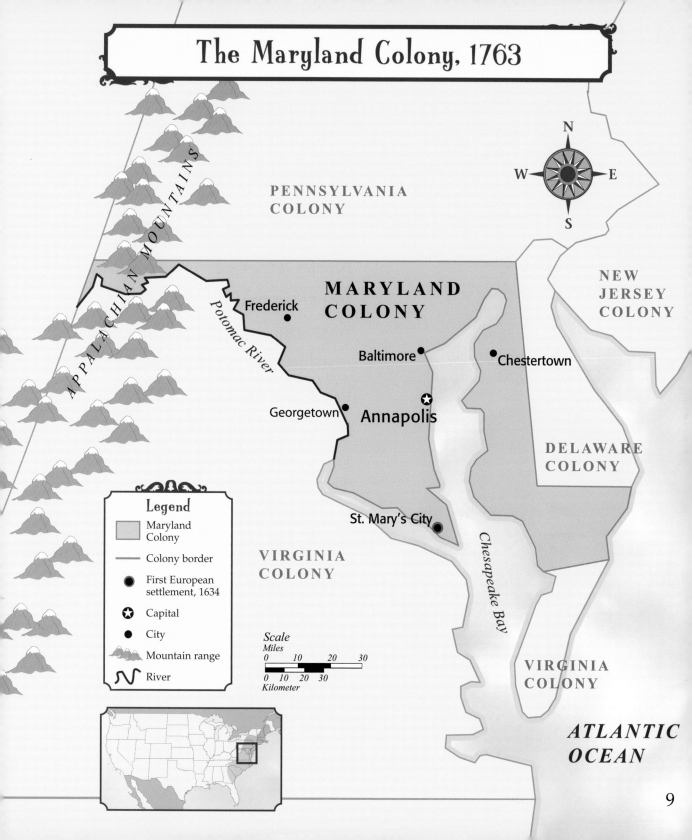

The Maryland Colony, 1763

PENNSYLVANIA COLONY

APPALACHIAN MOUNTAINS

Potomac River

Frederick

MARYLAND COLONY

Baltimore

Chestertown

NEW JERSEY COLONY

Georgetown

Annapolis

DELAWARE COLONY

St. Mary's City

VIRGINIA COLONY

Chesapeake Bay

VIRGINIA COLONY

ATLANTIC OCEAN

Legend

Maryland Colony

Colony border

● First European settlement, 1634

✪ Capital

● City

Mountain range

River

Scale
Miles
0   10   20   30
0   10   20   30
Kilometer

Cecilius Calvert followed his father's wishes and started a colony in North America. ▼

First Colonists

Cecilius Calvert sent his brother, Leonard, to start the new colony. In November 1633, two ships set sail for North America. The *Ark* and the *Dove* had a total of 200 passengers. Twenty Catholic **noblemen** were among the passengers.

Many of the passengers were **indentured servants**. The noblemen paid for the servants' trip. In return, the servants worked for a fixed number of years.

In March 1634, the ships arrived in the Maryland area. The settlers named their first settlement St. Mary's City.

After landing in Maryland, the first settlers gathered to worship at St. Mary's City.

More colonists came to Maryland in the following years. Most of them came to find religious freedom.

Maryland's growth changed the Algonquian way of life. Many Indians were forced off their land. Groups of Indians were forced to move north and south of Maryland. Many others became sick and died from diseases brought by Europeans.

Chapter 3

Colonial Life

Maryland was the sixth of America's 13 colonies. Colonial life was difficult. Colonists were starting over in a new land. They had to build houses, schools, and churches. Almost all supplies had to be shipped from Europe. Building projects were often delayed.

The settlers had to learn how to grow new crops. They cleared forests to plant small fields of corn and tobacco. Farmers grew fruits and vegetables to feed their families. They raised pigs and chickens. They also hunted and fished.

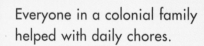
Everyone in a colonial family helped with daily chores.

13

▲ Clearing the land for settlement took a lot of work and time. The Algonquian shared their village with the early settlers.

Maryland settlers were not prepared for life in North America. The settlers discovered they could not grow the same grain crops they grew in England.

Settlers in North America also faced many new diseases, such as yellow fever. The settlers did not have good medicines to treat these illnesses. Many people died.

Growing Up

Colonial Maryland had few schools. Only the richest children went to school. Poor farmers could not afford to educate their children. Parents taught children to read. They wanted children to be able to read the Bible.

Children in Maryland worked hard. Girls helped their mothers pick vegetables, cook, and clean. Boys helped their fathers care for animals and crops.

Children helped their parents with work at home. ➡

~ Chapter 4 ~
Work and Trade

Maryland's **economy** depended on farming. Farmers grew most of their own food. Colonists grew squash and other crops. Maryland's soil was also good for growing tobacco. Tobacco sold for a high price in England.

Growing tobacco was hard work. Rich planters had indentured servants to help them grow tobacco. But the servants left when their time to serve was finished. Planters then had to find other help. In the 1680s, black people from Africa were shipped to Maryland to work as slaves. Slaves worked many hours in the tobacco fields for no pay.

Slaves were forced to work in Maryland's tobacco fields.

17

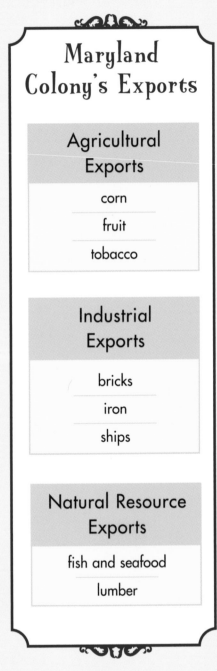

Maryland Colony's Exports

Agricultural Exports

corn

fruit

tobacco

Industrial Exports

bricks

iron

ships

Natural Resource Exports

fish and seafood

lumber

Planters were eager to get rich. They put many slaves to work in their tobacco fields. The added help meant larger crops and more money for the planters.

Some planters found other ways to make money. The colony had very few merchants. Planters bought supplies from merchants and soon opened their own stores.

Other Industries

Fishing was a growing industry in Maryland. People caught fish and seafood in the Chesapeake Bay. They sold the fish and seafood to other colonies and to England.

Maryland's land was rich in iron ore. In the early 1700s, colonists built factories to produce iron. People in Maryland's government saw how valuable iron was to the economy. In 1719, they passed a law to encourage the use of iron. People used iron to make cooking pots, tools, and building supplies. They also shipped iron ore to Europe.

Maryland, like each American colony, had its own money. ▼

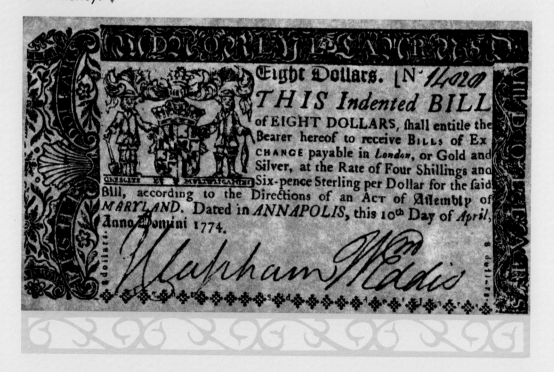

Chapter 5

Community and Faith

Some of the first American colonies were started for people of only one religious faith. These colonies passed laws punishing people who practiced a different religion. Maryland was different.

Welcoming Other Religions

The Calverts of Maryland wanted people of different faiths to work and live together. Most Maryland settlers felt the same way.

In 1649, Maryland's General Assembly passed the Act Concerning Religion. This law gave Christians the right to worship as they pleased.

In this painting by Tompkins Harrison Matteson, Maryland colonists adopt the Act Concerning Religion.

News of the Act Concerning Religion spread. People who were treated badly because of their religion heard about the freedom in Maryland.

Maryland's population quickly grew. People traveled from neighboring colonies and other countries to settle in Maryland.

Toleration Ends

By the late 1600s, the Act Concerning Religion began to lose force. The colony suffered from political troubles. Maryland's leaders changed several times. New leaders passed laws limiting religious freedom.

Population Growth of the Maryland Colony

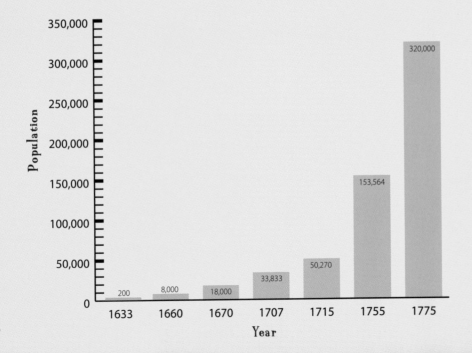

During the early 1700s, Catholics could no longer vote or hold any government offices. The early settlers' hopes for religious freedom in the Maryland Colony ended. Still, Maryland would be known as the first colony to pass a law for religious freedom.

Catholics often use beads when saying prayers. This part of a rosary was found at St. Mary's City. ▼

Chapter 6

Becoming a State

By the 1760s, the 13 American colonies had been settled for at least 150 years. The colonies had their own economies and ways of life. The colonists began to dislike Great Britain's control over them.

When the British taxed tea and paper, the colonists were angry. The people of Maryland thought the taxes were unfair.

In 1774, the colonies united and formed the Continental Congress. The colonies sent **representatives** to participate in the Continental Congress.

Maryland was the smallest of the Southern Colonies. ➡

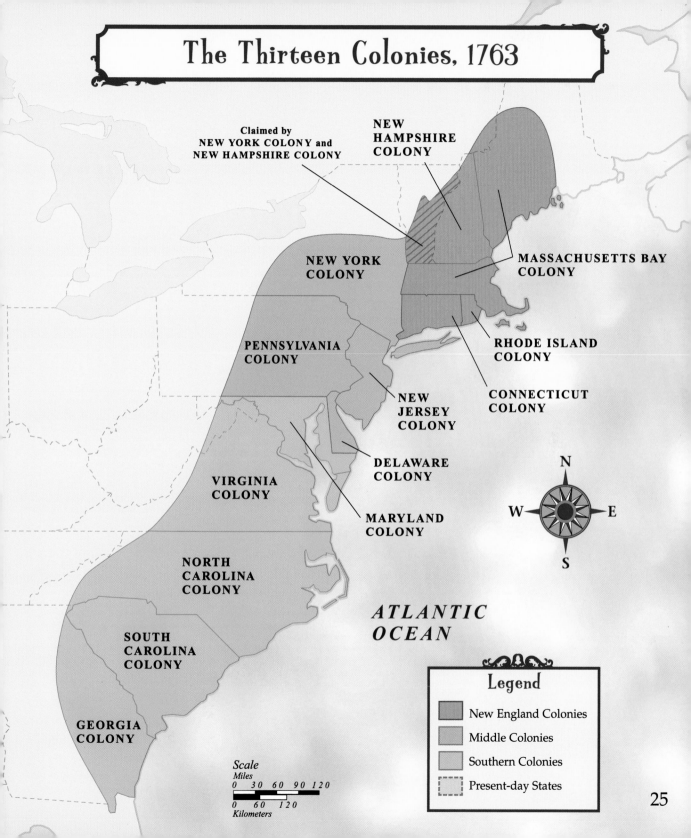

The Thirteen Colonies, 1763

Claimed by
NEW YORK COLONY and
NEW HAMPSHIRE COLONY

NEW
HAMPSHIRE
COLONY

NEW YORK
COLONY

MASSACHUSETTS BAY
COLONY

PENNSYLVANIA
COLONY

RHODE ISLAND
COLONY

NEW
JERSEY
COLONY

CONNECTICUT
COLONY

DELAWARE
COLONY

VIRGINIA
COLONY

MARYLAND
COLONY

NORTH
CAROLINA
COLONY

*ATLANTIC
OCEAN*

N
W E
S

SOUTH
CAROLINA
COLONY

GEORGIA
COLONY

Scale
Miles
0 30 60 90 120

0   60   120
Kilometers

Legend

New England Colonies
Middle Colonies
Southern Colonies
Present-day States

In July 1776, members of Congress approved the Declaration of Independence. This document declared the colonies independent states, free of British rule. Great Britain did not accept the declaration.

To gain their freedom, the colonies fought against Great Britain in the Revolutionary War (1775–1783). Both the colonists and the British used the Chesapeake Bay to transport soldiers and supplies. The United States won the war.

Following the war, Congress wanted to make its national government stronger. The U.S. **Constitution** united the states. On April 28, 1788, Maryland colonists adopted the constitution. It was the seventh state to join the United States.

◀ Colonists in Maryland forced an American ship owner to burn his ship, the *Peggy Stewart*. Colonists were angry because the ship owner paid British taxes for tea on the ship.

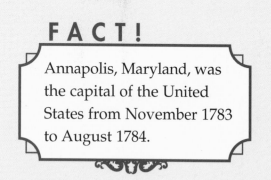

FACT!

Annapolis, Maryland, was the capital of the United States from November 1783 to August 1784.

Fast Facts

Name
The Maryland Colony
(named for Queen Henrietta
Maria, the wife of King Charles I)

Location
Southern colonies

Year of Founding
1634

First Settlement
St. Mary's City

Colony's Founders
George Calvert, Cecilius Calvert,
and Leonard Calvert

Religious Faiths
Catholic, Protestant

Agricultural Products
Corn, fish, fruit, seafood, tobacco

Major Industries
Fishing, ironworks

Population in 1775
320,000 people

Statehood
April 28, 1788
(7th state)

Time Line

1600s — 1700s

1649
Maryland Colony passes the Act Concerning Religion.

1634
Maryland's first settlement, St. Mary's City, is founded.

1707
An Act of Union unites England, Wales, and Scotland; they become the Kingdom of Great Britain.

1632
King Charles I grants charter to Cecilius Calvert for land that became Maryland.

1763
Proclamation of 1763 sets colonial borders and provides land for American Indians.

1719
Maryland Colony passes a law encouraging people to buy products made of iron.

1775-1783
American colonies fight for their independence from Great Britain in the Revolutionary War.

1715-1725
Iron is profitable in Maryland.

1783-1784
Annapolis, Maryland, serves as the nation's capital.

1788
On April 28, Maryland is the seventh state to join the United States.

1776
Declaration of Independence is approved in July.

Glossary

charter (CHAR-tur)—an official document that grants permission to start a city or colony and provides for a government

constitution (kon-stuh-TOO-shuhn)—the system of written laws in a state or country that state the rights of the people and the powers of the government

economy (e-KON-uh-mee)—the way a colony or a government runs its business, trade, and spending

indentured servant (in-DEN-churd SUR-vuhnt)—someone who agrees to work for another person for a certain length of time in exchange for travel expenses, food, or housing

nobleman (NOH-buhl-muhn)—a wealthy, upper-class person of high rank

palisade (pal-uh-SAYD)—a tall fence that protected an Algonquian village from animals and enemy attacks

representative (rep-ri-ZEN-tuh-tiv)—someone who is chosen to speak or act for others

Internet Sites

FactHound offers a safe, fun way to find Internet sites related to this book. All of the sites on FactHound have been researched by our staff.

Here's how:

1. Visit *www.facthound.com*
2. Type in this special code **0736826750** for age-appropriate sites. Or enter a search word related to this book for a more general search.
3. Click on the **Fetch It** button.

FactHound will fetch the best sites for you!

Read More

Burgan, Michael. *Maryland*. Life in the Thirteen Colonies. New York: Children's Press, 2004.

Jensen, Ann. *Leonard Calvert and the Maryland Adventure*. Centreville, Md.: Tidewater Publishers, 1998.

Williams, Jean Kinney. *The Maryland Colony*. Our Thirteen Colonies. Chanhassen, Minn.: Child's World, 2004.

Index